BE RESPECTFUL!

A HERO'S GUIDE TO BEING COURTEOUS

ELSIE OLSON

Consulting Editor, Diane Craig, M.A./Reading Specialist

Super Sandcastle

An Imprint of Abdo Publishing
abdobooks.com

abdobooks.com

Published by Abdo Publishing, a division of ABDO, PO Box 398166, Minneapolis, Minnesota 55439. Copyright © 2020 by Abdo Consulting Group, Inc. International copyrights reserved in all countries. No part of this book may be reproduced in any form without written permission from the publisher. Super SandCastle™ is a trademark and logo of Abdo Publishing.

Printed in the United States of America, North Mankato, Minnesota
052019
092019

Design: Sarah DeYoung, Mighty Media, Inc.
Production: Mighty Media, Inc.
Editor: Jessica Rusick
Cover Photographs: iStockphoto; Shutterstock Images
Interior Photographs: iStockphoto; Mighty Media, Inc.; Shutterstock Images

Library of Congress Control Number: 2018966956

Publisher's Cataloging-in-Publication Data
Names: Olson, Elsie, author.
Title: Be respectful!: a hero's guide to being courteous / by Elsie Olson
Other title: A hero's guide to being courteous
Description: Minneapolis, Minnesota : Abdo Publishing, 2020 | Series: Be your best you
Identifiers: ISBN 9781532119675 (lib. bdg.) | ISBN 9781532174438 (ebook)
Subjects: LCSH: Respect--Juvenile literature. | Courteous behavior--Juvenile literature. | Polite behavior-
    -Juvenile literature. | Manners--Juvenile literature. | Heroism--Juvenile literature.
Classification: DDC 177.1--dc23

Super SandCastle™ books are created by a team of professional educators, reading specialists, and content developers around five essential components—phonemic awareness, phonics, vocabulary, text comprehension, and fluency—to assist young readers as they develop reading skills and strategies and increase their general knowledge. All books are written, reviewed, and leveled for guided reading, early reading intervention, and Accelerated Reader™ programs for use in shared, guided, and independent reading and writing activities to support a balanced approach to literacy instruction.

CONTENTS

BE YOUR BEST YOU! 4

WHAT IS RESPECT? 6

BE COURTEOUS! 8

   SUPERPOWER! SAY PLEASE, PLEASE 10

   SUPERPOWER! HELP OUT 12

   SUPERPOWER! SAY IT NICELY 14

   SUPERPOWER! TOLERANCE 16

   SUPERPOWER! SAY YOU'RE SORRY 18

   SUPERPOWER! RESPECT YOURSELF 20

BE A HERO! 22

WHAT WOULD YOU DO? 23

GLOSSARY 24

ONLINE RESOURCES 24

BE YOUR BEST YOU!

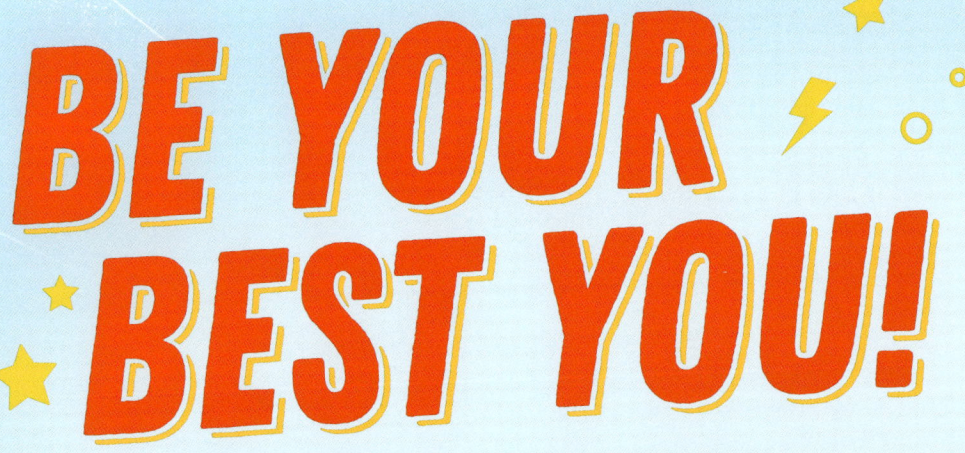

Have you ever done something that shows you care? Like saying please or thank you or offering to share?

Superheroes show respect to whomever they face. And this makes the world a more **courteous** place!

YOU HAVE THE POWER.
BE A HERO TOO.
BE RESPECTFUL OF OTHERS.

BE YOUR BEST
YOU!

WHAT IS RESPECT?

Respect is a lot like caring. It means showing that you think about how others are feeling. Respectful people are **courteous**. They have good manners. They help others.

BE COURTEOUS!

You can show respect everywhere you go! Just be **courteous**.

Some acts of courtesy are big. But even small acts of courtesy make a big difference! They make others feel cared about.

SUPERPOWER!

SAY PLEASE, PLEASE

Politeness is a superpower! It helps you show respect.

There is a simple secret to being polite. Just treat people the way you like to be treated.

GOOD MANNERS CHECKLIST

FOLLOW SIMPLE RULES TO ACT <u>POLITE</u>!

- ☐ Say please and thank you.
- ☐ Don't interrupt others.
- ☐ Say excuse me.
- ☐ Keep your mouth closed when chewing.

SUPERPOWER!

HELP OUT

Superheroes are all about action. Put your respect to work! Find small tasks you can do without being asked. When you help someone, they will be more likely to help out too.

SIX WAYS TO HELP OUT

★ Set the table for dinner.

★ Pick up trash outside.

★ Clean your room.

★ Tell your bus driver thank you.

★ Help a brother or sister with homework.

★ Make a card for a grandparent or neighbor.

SUPERPOWER!

SAY IT NICELY

Speaking is a superpower too. The things you say matter. They can make someone feel good or sad. So choose respectful words!

Say good morning. Tell your parent you love them. And say thank you to anyone who shows you kindness!

14

SHOW RESPECT ONLINE

Some people say mean things online. Before you post online, ask yourself:

WOULD YOU SAY THIS TO THE PERSON'S FACE?

WOULD YOU FEEL GOOD IF SOMEONE SAID THIS TO OR ABOUT YOU?

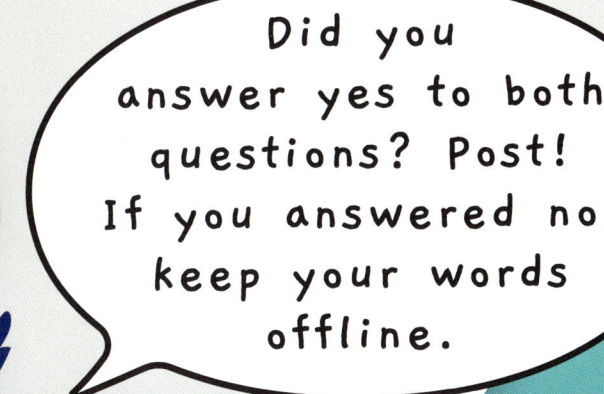

Did you answer yes to both questions? Post! If you answered no, keep your words offline.

SUPERPOWER!
TOLERANCE

Respectful heroes show **tolerance**. This means showing respect to people who are different from you.

16

SUPERPOWER!
SAY YOU'RE SORRY

Even superheroes make mistakes. But you have a superpower you can use when you mess up. It's **apologizing**!

It is hard to show respect all the time. Say sorry when you aren't respectful.

BE BRAVE

It can be scary to **apologize**. People may not forgive you right away. But apologizing is still the right thing to do.

SUPERPOWER!
RESPECT YOURSELF

Respecting others is important. But it is important to respect yourself too!

This means taking good care of yourself. Get lots of sleep. Eat healthy foods. And move your body every day!

BE A HERO!

It's your turn to take a stand. Act like a hero. Lend a hand.

With the words you say and the things you do, be respectful and **courteous**. Be your best you!

WHAT WOULD YOU DO?

Being a hero is about making respectful and **courteous** choices. How would you use your superpowers in the situations below?

You see your classmates making fun of a student who is dressed differently from others.

You accidentally break your sister's favorite toy.

You see your neighbor trying to carry many bags of groceries.

GLOSSARY

apologize – to say that you are sorry about something.

confidence – a feeling of faith in your own abilities.

courteous – showing respect toward others. Someone who is courteous shows courtesy.

polite – having good manners or showing consideration for others. Someone who is polite shows politeness.

tolerance – the ability to be accepting of people who are different from ourselves.

ONLINE RESOURCES

To learn more about being respectful and courteous, visit **abdobooklinks.com** or scan this QR code. These links are routinely monitored and updated to provide the most current information available.